IMAGES OF ENGLAND

FIRTH BROWN

A SHEFFIELD STEEL COMPANY

T0347061

Drop stamping jet discs at Firth Derihon's, Darley Dale in July 1954. Firth Derihon Ltd became well known for high quality stampings, particularly for the car and aircraft industries.

IMAGES OF ENGLAND

FIRTH BROWN

A SHEFFIELD STEEL COMPANY

CATHERINE HAMILTON

Acknowledgements

I would like to thank a number of ex-Firth Brown employees for their assistance in identifying and bringing to life many of the images in this book: George Holden, Keith Hutton, Peter Dakin, Les Steer, Donald Coddington, Alan Tunstill and Bob Conroy. I would also like to thank the staff of Kelham Island Museum for their patience while I have worked on this project.

First published 2000
Reprinted 2003, 2006

Reprinted in 2013 by
The History Press
The Mill, Brimscombe Port,
Stroud, Gloucestershire, GL5 2QG
www.thehistorypress.co.uk

© Catherine Hamilton, 2013

The right of Catherine Hamilton to be identified as the Author
of this work has been asserted in accordance with the
Copyrights, Designs and Patents Act 1988.

British Library Cataloguing in Publication Data.
A catalogue record for this book is available from the British Library.

ISBN 978 0 7524 1741 7

Typesetting and origination by Tempus Publishing Limited.
Printed in Great Britain.

Contents

Introduction

The Firth Brown company was formed in 1930 by the amalgamation of Thomas Firth & Sons and John Brown & Co. The photographs and illustrations within this book trace the development of the company and its associated companies from the 1850s through to the 1970s. Most of the images here are part of the Firth Brown Photographic Collection, housed at Kelham Island Museum in Sheffield, which was transferred from the Firth Brown Photographic Department when it closed in the 1980s. The collection is viewed as one of national importance as it records life in a huge Sheffield steel company from the 1930s through to the 1970s. Various subjects were chosen, everything from new pieces of equipment and products bound for Australia, to passport photographs of members of staff and Operatic Society pantomimes. The photographs show not only the working life of the company, but also the social life within Firth Brown's.

Thomas Firth & Sons

Thomas Firth and his two sons Mark and Thomas founded Thomas Firth's in 1842. Thomas Firth senior had a high reputation as a steel smelter, becoming head melter at Messrs Sanderson Bros & Co. His sons also worked there, with Mark taking up the commercial side and Thomas picking up more practical skills. However, the two sons became unhappy with their wages and decided to set up a business of their own. They started out in Charlotte Street, Sheffield in 1842 with just six crucible pot holes and persuaded their father to join them. Thomas Firth senior died in 1850.

They began as a small firm and gained a name for themselves in the production of high grade steels for items such as cutlery, shear and tool steels. As the years went by they expanded and purchased land in Savile Street. It was here that they built the 'Norfolk Works'.

When Thomas Firth senior died in 1850, Mark Firth became head of the firm and was assisted by his brothers Thomas and John. Their younger brothers Edward and Charles Henry later joined them in business. A Mr Gee remembers: 'Mr Mark (Firth) was a veritable Bismarck, ruling with a firm hand, working hard himself and expecting others to do likewise' (p.12, *The History of Firths*, Marshall & Newbould).

The company grew quickly with the construction of the new Norfolk Works and the Gun Works. They also acquired Clay Wheels Forges at Wadsley Bridge and Whittington Steel Works in Derbyshire. At the Whittington Works they produced double-storeyed corrugated steel railway carriages and telegraph posts for use in India.

Firth's was quick to adapt to new product lines. In 1856, when women were beginning to wear crinoline skirts, Firth's laid down a special plant to roll steel for the hoops. Just before demand for these came to a stop, all the machinery was cleverly sold to another firm.

Firth's also became well known for its production of armaments, particularly shells. The company set up huge Nasmyth hammers capable of forging tubes for large guns and producing steel shot. In 1863 they expanded again, with the construction of 25-ton hammers and the development of the 'Gun Works'. This later became known as the 'West Gun Works'.

Before 1860, no gun heavier than 68 pounds had been mounted on board a ship. During the 1870s the company forged guns of 35, 38, 75, 80 and 100 tons. This really was a huge advance in armament and gun manufacture. In 1871 the famous 'Woolwich Infant' was completed. It weighed 35 tons and could throw 700lb. of shot but this was surpassed two years later by a 38-ton 800 pounder.

Thomas Firth junior died in 1860 at the age of thirty-eight. During the 1870s Mark Firth was head of affairs, assisted by his brothers. Mark Firth was a well-respected director and had an active interest in the formation of the Iron and Steel Institute, set up in 1869, for which he was elected Master Cutler for three years in succession. He also supported his local community and built almshouses for the elderly on land at Ranmoor.

By this time Thomas Firth & Sons employed over 1,000 men and had become possibly the best known steel and gun forging firm in the world. Mark Firth hosted a visit from the Prince and Princess of Wales when they opened Firth Park, land that Mark Firth had purchased to be given to the people of his city. He also founded Firth College, later to become part of the University of Sheffield.

By the 1880s the firm had agents throughout Europe, North and South America, Africa and the Far East. Firth's employed nearly 2,000 men and its site covered twenty acres of land. A decade later the works consisted of Norfolk Steel Works, Shot Forge, Foundry and File, Saw and Edge Tools Works. Between them the various works produced 5,000 to 6,000 tons of crucible steel each year. This was used for general engineering work such as turning tools, twist drills, reamers, punches and hammers. Die blocks for stamping out drop forgings, parts of small arms, bicycles and sewing machines were also made in large quantities. In the rolling mills at the Norfolk Works, 15 gangs of men worked night and day to produce sheets for circular and other saws, cylinder laggings, shovels and bars for tools, drills and cutlery.

Just after 1900, the offices at the Norfolk Works were extended. In 1907 and 1908 new works were built at Weedon Street in Tinsley. The crucible steel department and rolling mills were moved there from the Norfolk Works.

Prior to the outbreak of the First World War, the firm's sites covered 44 acres and employed 3,000 men and just over 100 women. At the outbreak of the war however, extensions were made to the firm and 8,000 workers were on the payroll. Of these, 2,500 were women. In 1915 the government entrusted Thomas Firth & Sons with the erection and management of a National Projectile Factory at Templeborough where 5,000 women workers were employed. During the four and a half years of war, over four million shells were produced. The firm also supplied two million steel helmets.

John Brown & Co.

John Brown was born in Havell's Yard, Fargate in Sheffield on 6 December 1816. He started work at a firm of merchants, Earle Horton & Co. at the age of fourteen and later became a salesman for that company, which gave him the opportunity to travel the country. The company had by this time moved into the steel trade, manufacturing files and cutlery. Becoming more confident, Brown decided to make his own steel and set up his first works in Orchard Street, later moving to the Atlas Steel Works in Furnival Street. His first products were crucible steel files.

In 1848 Brown patented the conical spring and buffer, a product which stopped railway carriages crashing together. This invention was to be the root of John Brown's success and by 1853 he had works in four districts of Sheffield. A year later he decided to amalgamate all processes and purchased the Queens Works in Savile Street, a three acre site. It was renamed the Atlas Works and opened in 1856.

In 1858 Henry Bessemer set up works in Carlisle Street, next to John Brown's, where he used his new process to produce relatively cheap steel in large quantities. John Brown soon became interested in this and after some initial problems became one of the country's main producers of Bessemer Steel. By 1865 Brown was manufacturing around half the country's rail requirements

Brown's next endeavour was the improvement and production of armour plate for warships. In 1862 he won a gold medal at the London Exhibition for this work. The Royal Commission on Armour Plate placed most of their orders with John Brown. The business grew rapidly, employing 200 men in 1857 and 4,000 ten years later. It became a limited company in 1864.

Like Thomas Firth, Brown was also a prominent individual in Sheffield. He was Mayor in

1861 and a Town Trustee in 1864. He contributed to many churches and was elected chairman of the new Sheffield School Board in 1870. He was Master Cutler in 1865 and 1866.

During the 1870s the company struggled as armour plate production declined and steel rails were being produced more cheaply elsewhere. In 1879 the company paid out no dividends. But there were improvements during the 1880s with the invention of compound armour plate by J.D. Ellis and the erection in 1886 of a large forging press for making heavy forgings for guns and marine shaftings. In 1899 John Brown's purchased J. & G. Thomson of Clydebank and continued the production of ships there.

In 1915, during the First World War, John Brown's works came under government control to produce steel for the war effort. Production at Clydebank was extremely high with the completion of various battle cruisers and destroyers.

After the war, in 1919, John Brown's purchased Cravens Railway Carriage and Wagon Company at Darnall, Sheffield. They could then guarantee an outlet for their tyres, axles and springs.

During the 1920s the company once again struggled. Orders for armour plate fell, foreign competition from Belgium and Germany was strong and there were three strikes. In 1921 a new tyre mill and spring shop were both opened but employment was extremely low. At the end of the 1920s production at the Atlas Works did show some improvement with the start of manufacture of hollow-forged boiler drums for power stations. However there were still financial problems and a scheme was devised to rationalise sections of the company's business. The company was sold and transferred to Thomas Firth & Sons Ltd all of its Atlas and Scunthorpe works, thus amalgamating Thomas Firth and John Brown into 'Firth Brown'.

The photographs and illustrations which follow mainly show the firms after they amalgamated to form Firth Brown. The company continued to produce high quality steel castings and forgings for various industries in this country and around the world. As well as its Sheffield works, Firth Brown also had associated branches at Clydebank, Scunthorpe and Darnall, all of which are represented in these images.

One

Thomas Firth
and John Brown

Both founders of the two original steel firms (later to become Firth Brown) were well-respected businessmen of Sheffield. John Brown retired from his company in 1871. He did have other interests but stated he would not set up any other firm within fifty miles of Sheffield for ten years. However, in 1870, he assisted his nephew George Brown in the foundation of Brown, Bayley and Dixon. This company competed directly with his old firm. His wife, Mary, died in 1881 and Brown was devastated. He became ill and eventually left Sheffield while his mansion, Endcliffe Hall, was sold. He died after a further illness on 27 December 1896 in Bromley, Kent.

Thomas Firth died in 1850, so it was really his son Mark who managed Thomas Firth & Sons in its early years. By the 1870s Mark was a major public figure in Sheffield. He hosted a royal visit to Sheffield by the Prince and Princess of Wales, which naturally included a trip around his Norfolk Works. Mark continued working until his death, which came after he suffered a stroke on 16 November 1880. A carriage took him from the works to his home. Machinery at Thomas Firth & Sons was stopped. The interest in his welfare was so strong that special bulletins had to be put in the newspaper offices' windows each morning informing the public as to his health. He died on 28 November. All the firm's employees attended his funeral at the General Cemetery. The procession was said to be two miles long.

Thomas Firth. Born in 1789, died in 1850.

Sir John Brown
1816 - 1896

John Brown. Born in 1816, died in 1896.

10

An advertisement for the products of Thomas Firth & Sons. At the time of this advertisement, in the 1860s, the company was receiving many orders for railway products, due to the great expansion of the railways in Great Britain and the rest of the world.

An illustration from the Illustrated London News of August 1875. The royal visitors, the Prince and Princess of Wales, look on from a specially constructed stage while steelworkers teem crucible steel into ingot moulds. The process was a skilled one, originally invented by Benjamin Huntsman in 1742 while he was searching for a high quality steel from which to make watch parts.

ATLAS STEEL & IRON WORKS,
SHEFFIELD.

JOHN BROWN & CO.
(LIMITED),

MANUFACTURERS OF

ARMOUR-PLATES,

BOLTS, &c.,

𝔍𝔯𝔬𝔫 & 𝔖𝔱𝔢𝔢𝔩 𝔓𝔩𝔞𝔱𝔢𝔰,

FOR THE

BRITISH & FOREIGN GOVERNMENTS,

FOR BOILER, AGRICULTURAL IMPLEMENT
MAKERS, &c.

ATLAS MILD STEEL PLATES,

BEAMS, ANGLES, &c.

(TO STAND THE ADMIRALTY AND LLOYD'S TESTS.)

An advertisement for the products of John Brown & Co. They were also producing material for the railways as well as armour plate – for which they were to become well known. In the top left corner of the advert is the Atlas trademark of the firm.

THOS. FIRTH & SONS, LIMITED.

NORFOLK WORKS, SHEFFIELD.

Converters and Refiners of Steel.

Manufacturers of Genuine Double Refined CAST STEEL FOR AXES, EDGE TOOLS, SAWS, FILES, MACHINERY, and for every other purpose.

ALSO GENUINE BLISTERED STEEL, SHEAR, GERMAN FAGGOT, SPRING, &C. IMPROVED CAST STEEL FOR LOCOMOTIVE RAILWAY & CARRIAGE SPRINGS.

AND Manufacturers of every description of FILES, SAWS, & EDGE-TOOLS, WARRANTED.

The first page from an illustrated price list for Thomas Firth & Sons. The illustration shows the Norfolk Works in Savile Street, Sheffield. This was completed around 1852. Just before the new works opened, the firm held a huge dinner for all the workers, in the space that would become the sheet-mill. Mr John D. Thompson remembered, 'after the dinner there were plenty of long pipes, plenty of tobacco and beer, some speeches, and much clapping and hurrahing, and we all declared it was the grandest dinner that had ever been given to workmen.' (Marshall & Newbould 1924: p11).

14

Two

Factories and Sites

Latterly, the Firth Brown company occupied a huge site in the East End of Sheffield. However, to begin with both the John Brown company and Thomas Firth & Sons started their businesses on smaller sites. During the 1860s both firms expanded their sites and equipment considerably. In 1860 John Brown installed the first Bessemer Converter in Sheffield and in 1863 he erected a new armour plate plant. In 1864 Thomas Firth & Sons erected two 25-ton steam hammers and extended the crucible melting department to 360 crucible holes.

The two firms carried on with their developments over the years and in 1888 Firth's erected a steel foundry and a 3,000 ton forging press. In 1895 John Brown & Co. Ltd erected a new 10,000 ton armour forging press, a new armour rolling mill and an 8,000 ton armour bending press.

Expansion also meant purchasing other companies. In 1899 John Brown & Co. purchased the Clydebank Engineering and Shipbuilding Company. In 1901 Firth's opened a file factory at Riga in Russia and in 1904 they acquired the Salamander Works in Riga. Back in Sheffield, they built an additional works at Tinsley (1907). Both firms carried on growing as business boomed. Brown's steel foundry moved to Scunthorpe in 1918 and in 1919 Firth-Derihon Stampings Ltd was formed to take over the production of drop forgings. At the same time Firth's undertook substantial extension to the Engineers' Tool Department, the forge and Tinsley Works.

After the firms amalgamated in 1930 various changes were made to their respective sites. In 1934 Firth Brown engineers' tools department was entirely rebuilt on a new site. Two years later the company acquired portions of the Cyclops Works and laid down new bar rolling mills and bar heat treatment and finishing shops. In 1946 a separate tool steel department was set up in large new premises.

After the Second World War, Firth Brown acquired a Canadian distribution facility, made its tools division into a separate company, known as Firth Brown Tools Ltd, bought the Coventry machine tool firm of Wickman and established a separate engineering division around the production of mechanical presses and rolling mill parts.

During the 1960s and 1970s Firth Brown went through many restructuring regimes. By the 1980s there was a dramatic decline in the forging industry. In 1982 Firth Brown and Johnson merged its steelmaking interests with the British Steel Corporation's River Don Works to form a new company – Sheffield Forgemasters.

John Brown's Queens Works. In 1853 his works occupied four different sites, but in 1854 the Queens Works in Savile Street were offered for sale. John Brown purchased them for less than half they had cost to build. The works stretched from Savile Street to the Midland Railway line. Note the Queen's Head mounted as a keystone over the arch to the works – this can now be seen at Kelham Island Museum, Sheffield.

Firth Brown's Atlas Works, pictured sometime before 1940. The view was taken from the research building's roof. The large building on the left was the electric melting shop. In the foreground are houses that were later demolished. After Thomas Firth & Sons and John Brown & Co. amalgamated in 1930 various changes were made to their sites. In 1934 Firth Brown engineers' tools department was entirely rebuilt on a new site. Two years later the company acquired portions of the Cyclops Works and laid down new bar rolling mills, bar heat treatment and finishing shops.

A view of Firth Brown's works in March 1948. The view looks over to All Saints Church (known as 'John Brown's Church'). The soot from the works in the valley often hit washing on the lines of the houses behind in Grimesthorpe.

A view from the top of a chimney in 1948. It seems to be early morning and the smoke is probably caused by the tapping of a furnace. The pub on the left eventually closed down and became Firth Brown offices.

A general view of the tyre warehouse in 1949. To take this photograph the photographer would have climbed up onto something high, usually a vertical ladder to the crane track. He would have been carrying a large plate camera and a tripod.

The Norfolk bar rolling mills in July 1951. This was at Number One Gate, the beginnings of the massive Firth Brown site. Mr Norman Howard was the manager of the warehouse. It was one of the few areas where women worked at Firth Brown's. Here (on the left) they can be seen inspecting the bars. Elsewhere in the works women worked in the crane boxes.

Carlisle Street and Forncett Street. The pub on the corner is the Carwood. To the left of this is Gate 12 that led into the tyre mill. The building on the right is the joiners shop. Mr Alan Tunstill (photographic department) remembers taking progress photographs of the building towards the top end of the road.

A view over Firth Brown's roof tops. This one was taken from a watertower in August 1967.

The bar warehouse at Firth Derihon's, Darley Dale taken in June 1958. Each bar was numbered with a unique customer number.

Here bars are arriving at Firth Derihon's, Darley Dale in February 1959. Mr Vanpleu was in charge of the lorry garage. These black forged bars would probably be made into turbine discs for jet engines.

A general view of Firth Derihon's works at Darley Dale in 1959.

This shows the railway line running through the Firth Brown site in 1961. It was originally the first railway line to run from Sheffield to Rotherham and became a goods line for the Wicker Goods Yard. It was an important means of communication for Firth Brown. The Firth Brown Tools building is on the left. There was a passageway underneath the railway line to the other side. The railway still belonged to British Rail at this time so it was forbidden to cross. The building on the right of the picture is the Norfolk melting shop.

The new research building entrance hall and canopy in 1966. The creep laboratory was on the ground floor and the chemical and corrosion laboratories were on the top floor of the building.

The new office block at Firth Derihon's in 1969.

Three

Making Steel

Both John Brown and Thomas Firth began their businesses by making steel in order to produce specific products. Brown started his business making files and later railway springs, while Firth began by setting up a six pot hole crucible furnace and produced cutlery and tool steels. Both firms carried on producing the steel to make their products and did so after their amalgamation.

In 1860 John Brown & Co. was the first manufacturer to make rails from Bessemer steel. In 1871 chromium steel was made at the Atlas Works for the first time in England. In 1879 Brown's adopted the new Siemens furnaces for steel melting, followed by Firth's in 1884. In 1890 Firth's annual output of crucible steel amounted to between 5,000 and 6,000 tons. In 1900 Firth's began to manufacture high-speed tool steel and by 1902 made 40,000 tons of steel a year. The discovery of stainless steel in 1913 led to a revolution in steel products and 'Staybrite' corrosion resistant steels were developed in the Brown-Firth Research Laboratories ten years later.

In 1934 Firth Brown abandoned the production of crucible steel and also installed a new high frequency melting furnace. Research and development within the firm led to the production of various high quality steels, something the firm was well known for.

A Bessemer converter at the Scunthorpe Foundry in February 1949. Here metal is being poured into the converter prior to blowing.

Another Bessemer converter at the Scunthorpe site. This shows the next step in the process when the Bessemer is 'blowing'. Oxygen is added to the molten steel and creates the spectacular firework-like effects.

Tapping a high frequency furnace in February 1954. This was on the Norfolk Site where tool steels and stainless steels were produced. Firth Brown's often produced steel to accommodate their customers' particular requests rather than simply supplying a basic range of steels. Horace Green is on the left. The man on the right is the ladle man.

Tapping an electric arc furnace in April 1957. Here the ladle man is stopping the ladle from twisting around with the force of the stream of hot metal. The ladle is a small E6 bucket type ladle. The furnace man on the left is Jack Stanley.

The new practice of wearing safety helmets, pictured in August 1959. They were made of fibre glass and very heavy. The ingots here were 30 hundredweight ingots in the main Norfolk Shop. On the left is Harry Hall who worked at the Norfolk pitside melting shop. He eventually became a councillor for the Pitsmoor area and died in 1998. Joe Baldwin is in the centre.

The Norfolk melting shop, February 1960. This is a large ladle, weighing around 40 tons, operated by a 100 ton crane. Alf Sedgewick, right, the pyrometer man, takes a temperature reading while a forging ingot is cast. The man in the centre in a trilby hat is Charlie Waddle, the sample passer. Georgie Brown is on the right, making sure the lifters are correctly inserted.

Tapping the E6 electric arc furnace in March 1960. Here alloys such as titanium are being added while the tapping takes place.

Preparation for vacuum melting. Equipment for this process had to be extremely clean and even the scrap which went to be melted was cleaned first. The steel produced by vacuum melting was very high quality and was used mainly in aircraft parts. This photograph was taken in March 1962.

'Rabbling' the E3 melting furnace in July 1965. 'Rabbling' is the term for pulling the slag off the top of the molten steel. Here Bill Placket can be seen using a long rod with a wooden block on the end. It was heavy and hot work – a very skilled job.

Four

Shaping Steel

As the Firth Brown company grew, so did their range of processes and products. More works were constructed, allowing them to install larger furnaces, steam hammers and presses.

Other companies developed from the main arm of the firm. John Browns still existed on Clydebank where ships such as the Queen Mary were constructed. In 1917 John Brown & Co. moved their steel foundry from the Atlas Works to a site near Scunthorpe and a large number of work people and their families moved to the Scunthorpe area. The foundry produced steel castings, particularly for the grinding and crushing industries.

Firth Vickers was set up in 1934 for the production of stainless steels. Demand for stainless steel was incredibly high during the 1930s and without a large investment in new equipment Firth Brown would have been in difficulties. The English Steel Corporation stepped in, suggested a deal and invested heavily in the firm. Production was based at Firth's Tinsley Works in Weedon Street.

Firth Derihon combined two great steel names. The Derihon name was from a Belgian steelmaking family – they had set up their firm in 1857 in Liege for the production of high grade steel. The family fled to England before the First World War and in 1919 decided to stay. They officially combined with Thomas Firth & Sons to form Firth Derihon Stampings. They had three main factories in Sheffield – the old Tinsley works in Sheffield Road, the new works at Darley Dale and the Dunlop Street works which specialised in the forging of 'Nimonic' nickel alloy. In 1942 Firth Derihon produced the first set of drop forged turbine blades for the Whittle Gas Turbine.

A drop stamp machine, c.1940.

The engineers' small tool department at Firth Brown's, pictured in 1937.

Another view of the engineers' small tool department in 1937. The tool industry remained important in Sheffield and was an area where steel firms had close links. As well as segmented saws and files, the tool department developed tools for the watch making and instrument industries.

A workshop in the engineers' small tool department in 1937. This department eventually became Firth Brown Tools Ltd and in the 1950s introduced a new kind of tool – the 'Surform'. It was a cross between a rasp and a plane and could be used for the quick smoothing of wood or soft metal. The works manager, Mr Booth, developed the Surform.

A spring oil quenching machine at the spring shop in February 1939. Spring manufacture was a major process for the firm in the early years of the twentieth century when railways across the world were still expanding.

Women munitions workers in the East Shell Works in March 1941. Firth Brown contributed strongly to the 'war effort' in Great Britain between 1939 and 1945. The Atlas Works produced around half a million armour piercing shells and bombs; one million centrispun aero sleeves for Bristol engines; over 60,000 tons of armour plate for ships and tanks; nearly half a million forgings and 150,000 tons of special steels for aircraft.

Surfacing files prior to cutting, March 1941. While many male workers at Firth Brown were conscripted into the forces, women carried out many of their tasks in the factories of Sheffield.

Woman operating a 450-ton press in the Carbide Department. Women were also employed during the First World War. A quote from *The History of Firth's* by A.C. Marshall and Herbert Newbould (1924) states: 'The splendid tradition of Firth's for good relations between employers and employees were all maintained through the war. An outstanding feature, however, in Firth's as elsewhere, was the remarkable work done by female labour. Whether in the works – in front of a furnace, cleaning windows, forging shells under the presses or machining them in the lathes – or in the offices – fingering a typewriter, and keeping books, or assisting in the supervision of the workers – all of them right royally performed their allotted tasks. And in many ways, they helped to raise the tone of the workshops.'

A difficult shrinking operation in the north treatment – a view showing the shaft being placed in position. The man on the left is Stan Thatam (remembered for his pipe smoking). On the right Mr Robinson is checking the job. He is remembered for his brown suit and trilby. The photograph was taken in April 1949.

Metal spraying of a drum in Number 3 machine shop in October 1950. This was done when items were slightly undersized. The foreman in the picture could be Ernest Askew. Donald Coddington, an employee at the works, remembers shifting the 100 foot double-ended lathe with eight saddles when he was an apprentice.

A milling mechanic operator at Firth Brown Tools in February 1952. In 1934 Firth Brown's opened a new engineers' tool factory on Carlisle Street where they produced 'Insto' saws, 'Millenicut' files and 'Speedicut' high speed tools. The separate Firth Brown Tools Ltd was founded in 1946.

A tool and gauge fitter at Firth Brown Tools pictured in February 1952.

A draughtsman at Firth Brown Tools in February 1952.

Drop stamping discs at Firth Derihon's, Darley Dale, in November 1953. Firth Derihon Stampings Ltd was formed to take over the production of drop forgings in 1919.

Forging rings in the light forge at Firth Brown's in April 1953. This process required three men – one to work the hammer, one to take the weight of the forging and one to move it underneath the hammer.

Hammer forging a die block at Firth Brown's in May 1953. This task also required a high level of teamwork.

Tyre finishing and measuring photographed in November 1954. Other rolled products included carbon and alloy steel billets, bars and slabs, high-speed carbon and alloy tool and die steels, rings and steel plates.

A cold drawing operation being carried out on a 500-ton horizontal hydraulic draw bench in November 1955. The pipe, with the end partly closed down, is threaded on to a mandrel and a die is fixed in the moving cross head of the press, then drawn over it to decrease its wall thickness and increase its length. After drawing the pipe is removed from the mandrel in a reeling machine. The cold drawing process produces high quality surface conditions and precise dimensions.

Drop forging on a 5-ton hammer taking place at Firth Derihon's, Darley Dale in May 1956.

Workers forging a shaft on the upsetting hammer at Firth Derihon's, Darley Dale in May 1956. Note the clogs worn by the workers and the speed of the hammer caught on film by the photographer.

A new anvil block at Firth Derihon's Tinsley site in August 1957. This site was the former National Shell Factory and became a Firth Derihon site in 1919. Derihon's was a Belgian drop stamping company (Usines G. Derihon S.A.) which set up production in England during the First World War. They produced a large number of drop forgings from Firth's alloy steels. In 1919 they amalgamated to form Firth Derihon Ltd.

Working on a partly formed prepared piece or 'use' for a large steam turbine blade in November 1958. This was taking place at Firth Brown's, probably on the Savile Street side, an area known as 'down in the valley'. Here a small 5-ton hammer is worked by the hammer driver at the back. The forgeman is in the foreground and behind him is the barman, taking the weight of the metal held in the tongs.

Drop forging Nimonic at Firth Derihon's, Tinsley in December 1959. Nimonic is an extremely expensive type of steel containing 70% nickel and 20% chrome.

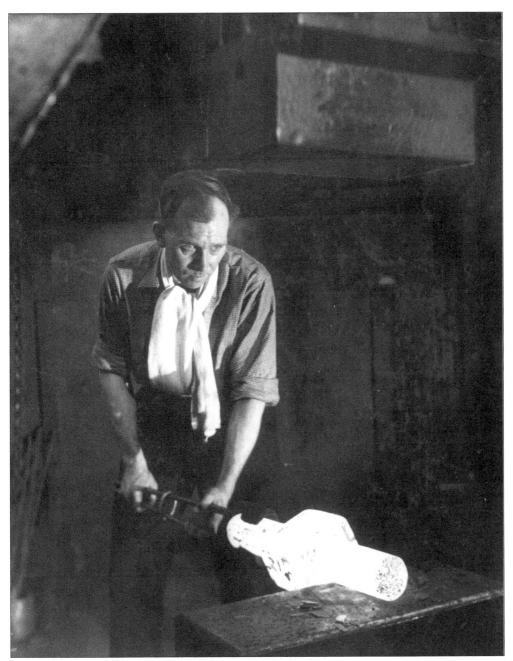

A forging smith at work in November 1959.

Gears being placed on a fabrication in 09 Shop in the heavy engineering department, September 1960. Apprentices are assisting with this process.

General view of the foundry at Firth Brown's Scunthorpe in February 1960. After Firth's old steel foundry closed, the trade in steel castings centred on the foundry that Brown's opened in Scunthorpe in 1918. This was expanded and a range of cupolas and side-blown converters were installed due to the increased trade.

The 'new' Bessemer Treatment shop, pictured in May 1961. The building here had replaced an older Bessemer shop. Rolls and arbours were heat treated here – they could stay inside the treatment furnaces for days or even weeks.

Forging a large turbine wheel in the 4000-ton press in October 1962. The foreman (wearing the lighter coloured coat) is possibly Bill Gommersall.

Grinding a thrust shaft in November 1967. Customers would request particular types of finish on their rolls. The man pictured here is Arthur Vausc.

The largest ever roll arbour under the 4000-ton press, September 1968.

Five

Products

Both founding firms were successful due to the type of products they originally made and the materials they used. John Brown began by making railway springs and Firth's started out making tool steels and cutlery. In 1849 Brown patented the conical spring buffer – the product he built the firm's success upon. Firth's forged their first gun in 1852. Brown's produced a 5-ton armour plate by rolling in 1861 – they were to become famous for this product. By the time John Brown finally retired in 1870 the products made by his company were incredibly varied and included iron boilers, ship and bridge plates, armour plate, Bessemer steel rails, tyres, axles and springs and various other forgings including ordnance.

While Brown's were developing stronger and stronger armour plate, Firth's were producing high quality guns. Their first gun was forged at Clay Wheel Forge in 1852 and by the 1870s Firth's had become the foremost gun forging firm in the world. Firth's pioneered the use of crucible steel for inner gun tubes in 1860. In 1871 they completed the 'Woolwich Infant' a 35-ton gun, followed at two year intervals by 75-ton and 80-ton guns.

In 1900 they developed armour-piercing shells to carry a bursting charge. In 1932 the Firth Brown company produced what was then the world's largest hollow-forged reaction vessel, 70 tons in weight, 50 feet long and 6 feet in diameter. Steel produced by the company was used within their various branches, such as at Clydebank for ships, at Cravens in Darnall for railway coaches and at Firth Brown Tools in Sheffield for various tools.

Later, the company produced carbon and alloy steel ingots and blooms for forgings. These forgings were used on land and marine turbines, marine transmission gear, heavy oil and gas engines and for electrical machinery. They also produced hollow-forged boiler-drums, chemical reaction chambers and oil-distillation vessels. Other forgings were used for railways, aircraft and motor-car manufacture. Carbon and alloy steel bars were produced for all types of machinery. Special steels such as magnetic steels and steels with a low thermal expansion were produced. The company also produced small tool products such as cutters, reamers, hacksaws and rasps. Carbon and alloy steel castings were made for agricultural machinery, bridge constructions, chemical plants, dredging and colliery equipment, railways and electrical plant. The following images show a number of these products.

A ground and polished roll in April 1939. These products were used by rolling mills and paper mills. They were also used on site to roll sheets. Many were made from carbon chrome steel. This one hasn't been polished up just for the photograph – they were always finished like this and required careful transporting.

A group of large springs and a worker in April 1939. John Brown & Co. produced large quantities of items for the railways, springs being one of them.

A steam and water drum bound for the 'Portsmouth Electricity Undertaking' in July 1940. Note the Pickfords road locomotive, made by John Fowler of Leeds.

Two ships, *Imperio* and *Rangatiki*, at John Brown's on Clydebank in April 1948. During the Second World War a large number of ships were produced at Clydebank. Ships including the Cunard White Star liner *Queen Elizabeth*; the battleship *Duke of York* and the battleship *Vanguard* were all produced by John Brown & Co.

A general view of railway springs in racks ready for dispatch in August 1949.

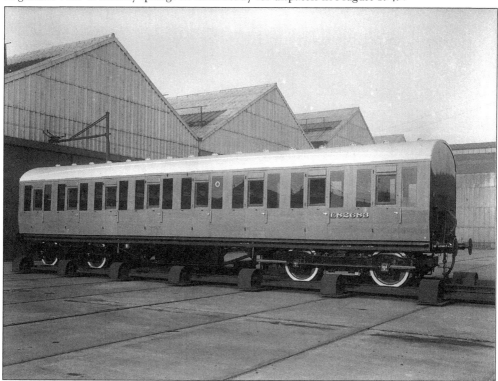

A passenger coach produced by Cravens in January 1949.

A Nigerian railway coach at Cravens in January 1949. Mr Alan Tunstill, a photographer at Firth Brown's, remembered many trips to Darnall to take photographs of the carriages. Cravens had a contract with the Crown Agents for the Colonies and built many carriages for countries such as Nigeria and Rhodesia. The Crown Agents were very particular about the photographs they would accept and wanted a side view and an end view of the carriages.

A 20-ton roll in new slings in the roll grinding shop in November 1953. These products were very accurately made.

A polished roll. This photograph was taken in February 1954 with the aim of showing the reflections produced by the fine finish.

A long roll in the roll grinding shop in April 1956. The foreman on the left is Wilf Aram – he later became the works manager.

Eric Yeatman machining a 90-ton forging for a vertical generator shaft in No. 3 machine shop in September 1957. The shaft was ordered by Metropolitan Vickers Co. Ltd for delivery to Bhakra in India.

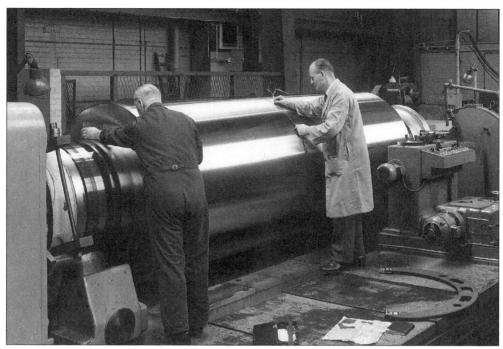

One of a pair of back up rolls for a huge plate mill in Sweden. It was made as a one piece forging and weighed around 45 tons. In February 1958 it was the largest forged back up roll Firth Brown's had made.

A tube and drum produced for a carpet company in Melbourne, Australia, April 1955. The man in photograph is Arthur Pugh.

The roll treatment department in April 1955. This was in the south section of Firth Brown's works. The furnaces here were between 25 and 30 feet deep. The treatment produced a hard surface and was very closely controlled to alter the structure of the steel, although the rolls sometimes exploded inside the furnace. It was a difficult job to pull them out as the pieces weighed around a quarter of a ton each.

A view of 3/4 machine shop in April 1955. The product is a ring for Westminster Carpets in Melbourne, Australia. On the right is the marking out table where rough castings were marked with white paint before they were machined. The marker here could be Keith Hutton who was an apprentice at the time.

Cooling blades for aircraft made from nimonic steel, a very specialised material.
The photograph dates from September 1956.

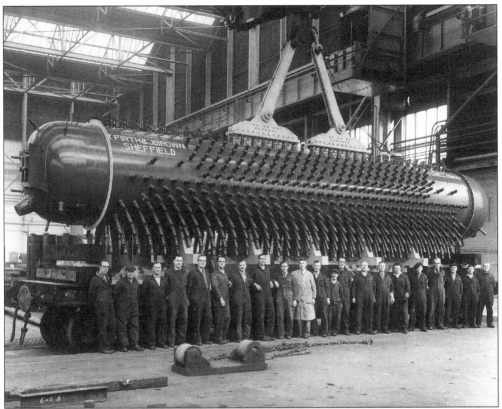

An 85-ton forged boiler drum produced for a generating station at Skelton Grange in January 1959. The drum was made by welding together two hollow-forged half drums, each with an integral closed end. It was fitted with 880 welded stub tubes and attachments and became known as 'the porcupine'. Workers from left to right: Jim Ward, Albert Massindew, Frank Pendall, Cyril Orry, Len Buckley, Stan Hinds, Johnny Hodgson, Frank Weston, Don Bingham, Tommy Hope, Harold Watson, George Carter, Bill Higgins, Bill Howard, Wilf Harrison, Alf Beech, Jack Clark, Harry Murphy, Joe Ironsides, Billy Higginbottom and Cyril Keeton.

Forged turbine discs in December 1960. The man here is helping to guide the disc as it is lowered into place.

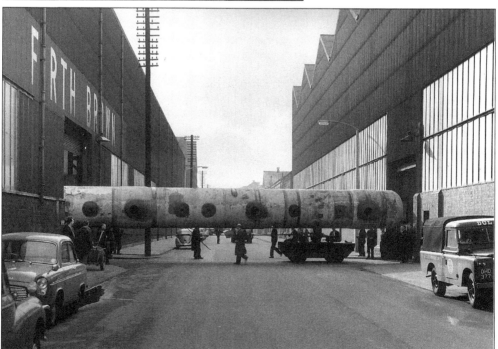

A Drakelow boiler drum being carried from 02 shop to 01 shop across Carlisle Street in October 1961. In the background on the right is the Corner Pin pub and in the distance the Firth Brown Tools works. The works has since been demolished.

Castings at the Scunthorpe foundry in April 1962.

A large diameter composite cast ring at the Scunthorpe Works in August 1968.

Grinding balls pictured at the Scunthorpe foundry in March 1962.

Workers checking the diameter of a large forged ring in the 4000-ton shop in July 1964.

In the tyre mill warehouse at the bottom of 12 Gate in March 1965. The man is checking the diameter of the tyre.

Large rings in the 3-4 machine shop in January 1969. Jack Wilson, pictured here, later became a foreman.

Coining press castings at the Scunthorpe foundry in the late 1960s.

Six

Firth Vickers and Stainless Steel

Stainless steel was discovered by Harry Brearley in the Brown-Firth Research Laboratories in 1913. While studying steel for gun barrels he tested low-carbon steels that contained only 12% chromium and found these steels had the ability to resist corrosion. Brearley recognised the commercial implications of the discovery and suggested the steel could be used for cutlery. Although his discovery was successful, there was some dispute over the rights to his invention and this eventually this led to his resignation from Firth's.

The 'Staybrite' brand of corrosion resistant steel was developed in 1923 by W.H. Hatfield. It was 18 per cent chromium and 8 per cent nickel and opened a massive new market for Firth's. Stainless steel could be used for a large number of products including kitchen sinks and shop fronts. The chemical industry was also a large user of stainless steel.

In 1934 'Staybrite' steel was on display at the *Daily Mail Ideal Homes Exhibition*. A brochure was produced containing images of products made from the steel. The brochure contained everything from letterboxes, cutlery and cake stands to brewing equipment, fish fryers and pressure vessels. One of the most famous ships to be built, *The Queen Mary*, was launched in 1934 and made use of a large amount of 'Staybrite' steel.

Firth-Vickers Stainless Steels Ltd was formed the same year when Firth Brown and the English Steel Corporation Ltd became equal partners.

During the Second World War stainless steel for domestic use was sacrificed for the war effort, and it was not until the late 1950s that this type of steel became plentiful again. It was once more used for a wide variety of products including furniture, kitchen equipment and building facings.

The 'Staybrite' ball at Barker's Pool Garden in Sheffield. The back of the cinema and the Grand Hotel can be seen in the background.

Assorted 'Staybrite' products in June 1943. This image was to be included in the Staybrite Dining Brochure. It was fairly difficult to photograph these types of objects because they were so shiny. The photographers used rolls of white paper or silk to reflect the light combined with cut outs of black paper to give a softer tone to the products.

The collection of stainless steel products known as the 'Staybrite Museum', located on the top floor of the Research Building. This photograph was taken before the building was damaged by the Blitz. Items here include cutlery, surgical instruments and kitchenware.

A later photograph of the collection of 'Staybrite' products. Items here include golf clubs, hand rails, furniture and fittings for ships. This 'museum' must have been reconstructed after the Second World War.

A breakfast set made from 'Staybrite' steel. This photograph was probably taken for publicity purposes. However it is interesting that it was taken in June 1941 when most stainless steel was being used for war-related products and its use for domestic items was rare. Note also the Firth Vickers logo on the tea service.

A fireplace in 'Staybrite' steel. During the 1930s stainless steel became a fashionable material for domestic furniture and fittings.

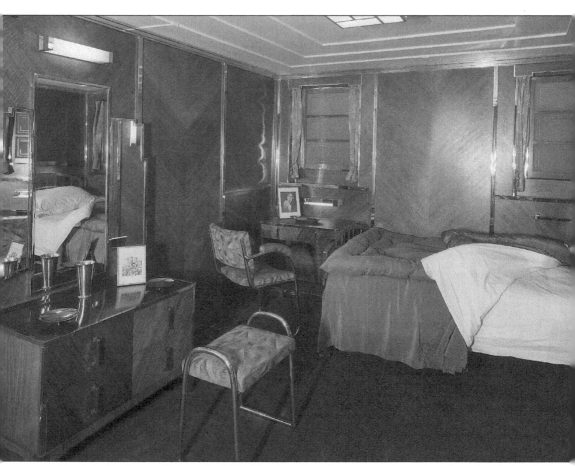

'Staybrite' bedroom fittings. In 1934 'Staybrite' steel was strongly marketed at the Daily Mail Ideal Homes Exhibition. A brochure was produced containing images of products made from the steel. In a description of uses of the steel within the home, the brochure states: 'The soft gleam of modern tubular "Staybrite" steel chair frames; the dressing table with its complement of, "Staybrite" Steel trays, Manicure Sets, Brushes and the many other toilet accessories, all bespeaking the inherent taste of the owner of beauty, utility and cleanliness. Curtain rails, lighting fittings and picture frames together with door furniture – in fact, the whole range of metal fittings are made of "Staybrite" Steel.'

Large 'Staybrite' pressings, pictured around 1940. Sheets of the steel would be pressed to form these shapes.

Descaling 'Staybrite' sheets in the old brewery yard in the 1940s.

The galley on HMS *Sheffield*, April 1939. HMS *Sheffield* was the City of Sheffield's first warship and was launched on 23 July 1936. All the fittings on board, which would usually be made of brass, were made of stainless steel. This was a trial to see if the steel would reduce the amount of work required by the crew in cleaning the brassware. The ship soon became known as the 'Shiny Sheff'.

HMS *Sheffield* in April 1939, this time showing the 'Staybrite' steel handrails.

The Firth Vickers strip mill in June 1939.

An early image showing stainless steel production around the early 1940s. A sheet of stainless steel has just gone through the rollers.

The Firth Vickers stand at the British Industries Fair at Castle Bromwich in the West Midlands in May 1948.

The hot mill at Firth Vickers' Weedon Street works, Tinsley, in September 1953.

The 'Staybrite' grill in Ellesmere Road post office in October 1953. This post office was close to 'John Brown's Church'.

The Robertson cold rolling mill at Weedon Street, Tinsley in September 1953.

Hot rolling mills at Weedon Street in May 1954. This image gives an idea of how quickly the metal was moving through the rollers.

The rolling mill team at Firth Vickers' Weedon Street works in August 1960. This was the last plate to be made in the hand mills.

Stainless steel centrispun tubes at Firth Vickers' foundry machine shop, Shepcote Lane, in the late 1960s.

Blow pipes for Appleby Frodingham being despatched in July 1960.

A product for the Snowy Mountain water turbines in Australia, May 1964.

The Firth Vickers stand at a trade exhibition at Olympia in London in 1965. Their main exhibit was a stainless steel plate 10 metres by 2 metres in diameter.

The Lord Mayor's Parade in Sheffield in 1968. Firth Vickers had a float which included stainless steel products such as cutlery and beer kegs.

Another Lord Mayor's Parade in the 1970s. Firth Vickers took part in the publicity campaign 'Sheffield – City on the Move' and their 'Staybrite' steel ball was often to be seen.

The 'Staybrite' steel ball, this time appearing at the Sheffield Corporation Parks Department exhibition in the Sheffield Show in 1972.

Seven

Research and Testing

Research has always been an important and integral part of steel production and the Brown-Firth Research Laboratories were founded in 1908. Here the two companies joined forces in applying science to their industries. Many discoveries were made here – for example the invention of stainless steel and the development of the 'Staybrite' brand, and work on Nitralloy steels. In 1939 spectrographic and radiographic departments were added to the laboratories. A year later, special steels for high temperature service, developed in the research laboratories, were supplied for key components of the early Whittle gas turbines. The research department housed various laboratories such as 'refractories', 'x-rays' and 'chemical analysis'. On the top floor of the building was a museum housing a collection of metallurgical exhibits.

In 1945 additional research premises were opened. These contained high frequency melting, electronic, creep testing and physical metallurgy departments. An electron microscope was installed. The research laboratories served not only Firth Brown's in Sheffield and the Scunthorpe foundry, but also Firth Vickers Stainless Steels Ltd and Firth Derihon Stampings Ltd. During the 1950s the Brown-Firth Research Laboratories continued as a major centre for steel research. Sir Charles Sykes took over from W.H. Hatfield in the research department. Although no major discoveries were made, progress continued in improving the properties of steel and modifications were made for the motor, chemical, aircraft and atomic energy industries. Research continued to give Firth Brown's a reputation for high quality special steels.

Mr Newton's general laboratory at Norfolk bar works in December 1938. The man on the left is George Smith, behind him is Bill Watkins and the man to his right is Harold Oldham. Mr Newton, the laboratory manager, always played golf on Saturdays and workers would wear plus fours in order to 'get in' with their boss. The old fume cupboards are on the right.

A general view of the research department micro laboratory in the 1940s. The doors at the back led to darkrooms. The laboratory overlooked the research yard and stainless steel foundry.

Testing railway springs in April 1941. Firth Brown's stopped producing these just after the Second World War.

The research library. Above the fireplace is a portrait of Dr W.H. Hatfield – the developer of 'Staybrite' steel. During the Second World War this room was used for firewatching.

Jack Lavender operating an electron microscope at Gower Street in June 1939. John Morley was in charge of this department.

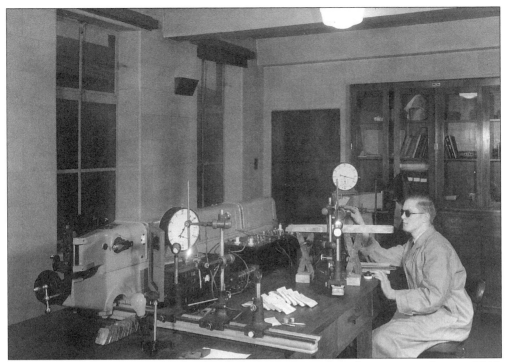

A general view of the spectrographic bench in the spectographics department in January 1940. This was in the old research laboratories in Princess Street.

A woman working in the research department during the Second World War.

The research laboratory in December 1940, the night after the Blitz struck Sheffield.

The spectrographic laboratory in 1942 where Herbert Shirley was in charge. This was over the x-ray laboratory in the research yard.

August 1949. An experimental high frequency furnace in the research department, probably at Gower Street. The man on the left of the furnace is possibly Andy Ardron.

Sulphur printing a cropped ingot in August 1951. Sensitised paper was soaked in sulphuric acid while the face of the ingot was prepared by fine machining. The paper was laid on top and the acid would reveal impurities.

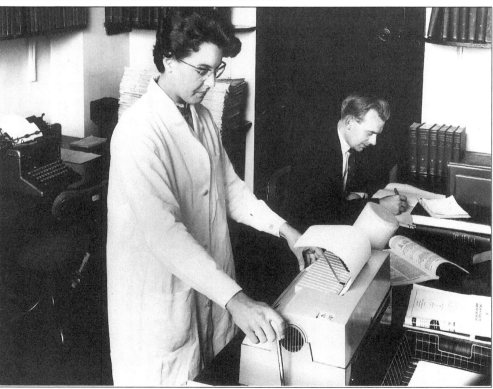

The Firth Brown Research Library in September 1960. The library held 4,000 books as well as subscriptions to over 100 periodicals, pamphlets and lantern slides.

The creep laboratory within the new research laboratories in March 1967. Machines in the creep laboratory are capable of detecting changes in extension of as little as five millionths of an inch. Firth Brown steels and Firth Derihon drop forgings were used in every British-engined aircraft and are prime examples of the end-use of special creep-resisting steels.

Experimental melting taking place during April 1967. This photograph was taken to go in a brochure about the research department at Firth Brown's.

A worker pictured using a micrometer to measure a 42in diameter roll in October 1954.

Supersonic testing the product in the research warehouse in March 1955.

Inspecting the end coupling on the low pressure rotor of a 200mw steam turbine that has been assembled for testing, January 1961.

Checking the diameter of a back up roll sleeve produced for Belgium in July 1962.

Shafts in the 3-4 machine shop in March 1962. The man on the left is testing the shafts for cracks while a visiting inspector from a customer company looks on. This photograph was taken before research staff wore white coats.

Eight

Photographic Department

It seems that the photographic department at Firth Brown's was set up some time during the 1930s. Index books which survive from the department date from December 1937. After 1945 the department was located downstairs in what had been the casualty clearing station during the Second World War. Mr Alan Tunstill joined the department after the war. Other staff were Mr Stan Thorpe, Mr Jack Dalton, Mr Reg Frost and two female printers. Photographers in the department were given jobs by various sections within the firm. Alan Tunstill, one of the works photographers, remembers a trip to Clydebank to take pictures of the launch of the *Coronia*, a trip to Dore Moor house, which was the Managing Director's residence, and trips to Darnall to see railway carriages at Cravens works. He remembers using cameras such as a super-iconta 120 with a Zeiss Tessa Lens during the 1950s and a Leica until the 1960s.

By 1977 the photographic department at Firth Brown's had been cut back to only two or three staff. It closed sometime between 1979 and 1980.

Taking a wide angle shot of a kitchen set-up in January 1943. Photographs were taken for publicity purposes as well as to provide a record of products and developments within the company. This photograph was probably for a brochure of 'Staybrite' kitchen equipment. It is interesting to note it was taken on 1 January, during the Second World War.

The photographic department office at Lerroy Street (between Savile and Princess Street) in July 1948.

Another image of the photographic department in 1948. Here Rita Horton and Pam Spencer (?) print up the negatives. It is possible they printed up this one.

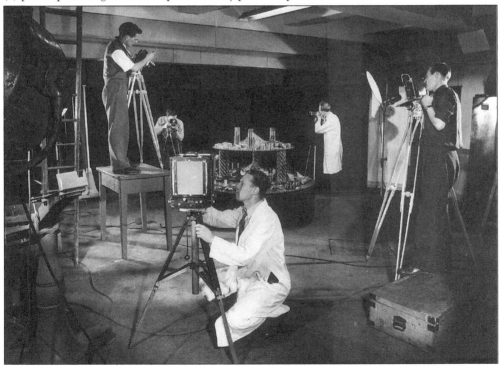

Taking photographs of Firth Brown Tools in the outer studio in June 1954. Before publicity and advertising departments expanded, the photographers themselves would arrange the products.

Large prints being loaded onto a lorry in May 1960. Prints like these went to exhibitions in places such as Mexico City, Liege and Barcelona. The print on the right shows the hydraulic press in 09 shop. This image also gives an idea of the location of the photographic department at Firth Brown's. On the right there was a ramp leading down into the department – it was like going into a dungeon. In the background is the 'directors' corridor'.

A large print in the photographic studio in June 1964. Jack Dalton is standing in the centre.

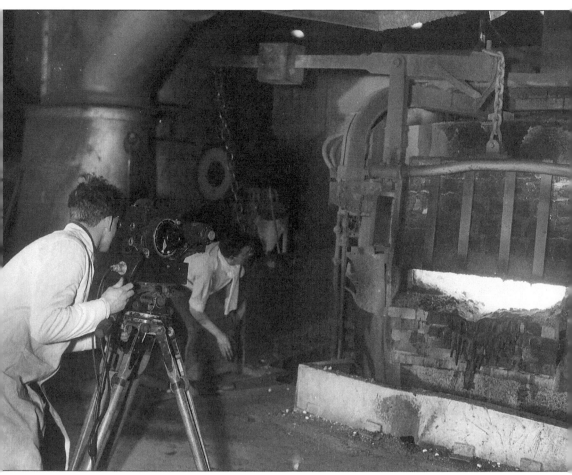

Using a high speed camera to take photographs in the Melting Shop in April 1967.

Nine

Learning the Trade

The Apprentice Training School opened in 1947 to provide boys with a basic training in the use of modern machine tools. By 1952 its machine shop had doubled in size. In 1945 there were just twelve boys training. By 1952 there were thirty.

From its beginnings in the 1940s the school became self-contained and comprised a workshop, tool stores, mess room and lecture room. After initial training here boys were taken step by step through various aspects of the trade at Firth Brown's.

Many employees of the firm went there straight from school and stayed for many years, if not for their whole working careers. Schools visited to look around the company, and a permanent display about Firth Brown's was erected at Granville College.

November 1953. On the right Charles Sykes, the Director of Research, presents an apprentice with a trophy. George May, the training officer, can be seen in the background.

An apprentice under instruction on a lathe in the Apprentice Training School. Syd May, the training instructor, is on the left. The picture dates from January 1956.

Apprentices in the Atherton Room in September 1957. This was in the new Apprentice Training School which boasted facilities including a workshop, reception area and conference room.

Another photograph showing apprentices under instruction in the Atherton Room in October 1957.

An apprentice pictured being trained in March 1960.

A group of young apprentices at Norfolk bar rolling mills in October 1961.

Firth Brown display panels at Granville College in January 1962. School groups also visited the Firth Brown works in order to get an idea of what working in the steel industry would be like.

Boys sitting the basic training school entrance exam in July 1968.

Apprentices in the tool room within the Firth Brown Basic Training Centre in April 1968.

A general view looking over the Apprentice Training School in the late 1960s.

Ten

Staff, Visitors, Exhibitions and Pantomimes

As the founding firms grew, social activities for employees developed. The Atlas and Norfolk Works Sports Club was formed in 1903. By 1938 the club ran football, rugby, tennis, bowls, table tennis, billiards and swimming. There was also an Atlas and Norfolk Angling Club, a boys club and a Firth Brown and Firth Vickers Operatic Society founded in 1927. Departments would run their own trips every year. In the 1960s Mr Dakin remembers maintenance department day trips to Blackpool and Skegness and trips to the races, as well as other holidays. 'At Christmas time you would only get Christmas Day and Boxing Day off. The firm didn't put on any great "do". When they built the Atlas Melting Shop they did have a big do. But the workers on the furnaces were used to drinking. The youngest bloke in the crew would go off to the Carwood Pub. He'd take a brush handle lined up with twenty to thirty mash cans which would be filled with beer. This would happen two to three times each shift. This went on until the late 1960s. Beer was replaced by lime juices or salt solutions – to the disappointment of the workers...'

Alan Tunstill, a Firth Brown photographer, remembers accompanying works managers on an excursion to the Dales. 'Three coaches of men went first to York for coffee and then to Helmsley for lunch and eventually back to York for a huge dinner'. Alan was only twenty-one at the time and was amazed at the extravagance of the outing.

Mr Bob Conroy, a chemistry laboratory worker, remembers enjoying the camaraderie of work in the general laboratory. He attended staff dances, played hockey and was on the committee for the Atlas and Norfolk Sports Club.

The forging press team at John Brown & Co. in 1898.

Staff of the Engineers' Tools Department in 1912. This department later became
Firth Brown Tools Ltd. Note the age of the boys at the front.

An invitation to an ex-servicemens' dinner in November 1931. This illustration is from a copy of *The Bombshell*, a monthly journal for Firth Brown employees.

The BOMBSHELL

A Monthly Journal devoted to the interests of the employees of Thos. Firth & John Brown LIMITED, · SHEFFIELD ·

SAFETY FIRST

NORMAN BURKINSHAW.

No. 11.   Vol. 15.   November,   1931.   Twopence.

Staff of the Engineers' Tools Department in May 1934. From left to right, back row: J. Platts, B. Wainwright, W. Maddy, W. Wilson, F. Laycock, T. Traunter, C. Sharpe, S. Shepherd, J. Gingell. Third row: J.W. Moody, W. Druce, A.E. Perry, R. Staniforth, W. Thompson, W. Harrison, P. Parker, G. Godley, R. Mawson, J. Haigh, A. May, F. Lister. Second row: J. Hodkin, B.H. Frith, E. Kenny, W. Pringle, E. Taylor, J.H. Barber, W. Parkin, F. Bailey, H. Bingham, H. Pearson. Front row: W. Slack, J. Durkin, H. Williamson, E. Thompson, F. Kenny, A. Turner, A. Hinchcliffe, W. Starkey.

Previous page: The front cover of the November 1931 issue of *The Bombshell*. The March 1919 issue included a poem about the publication – Our 'Mag'

If you're in pain, but not insane
Just fly, to Mr Marshall
He'll give you the cure right quick he'll procure
The February 'Bombshell'.
Just read it through, I can tell you,
It's the latest thing in 'Mags',
You'll laugh at the wits, you'll scream at the skits,
While you smoke a packet of fags.
There's competitions in galore,
And beautiful love tales,
Photography and poetry,
Buy one and help the sales.

Workers pictured taking part in a staff show in 1935.

The works' cricket team from 1937.

Preparing for Christmas in the engineers' tools department during the 1940s.

The Duke of Kent's visit to Firth Brown's in July 1938. Dr. W.H. Hatfield can be seen in the centre. Various members of the royal family visited the company over the years. In 1875 the Prince and Princess of Wales (later King Edward VII and Queen Alexandra) visited the Norfolk Works. In 1915 the firm was visited by King George V and in 1941 by King George VI and Queen Elizabeth.

The presentation of football jerseys to members of the Atlas and Norfolk sports club in the 1930s.

Sir Allen Grant presenting a cheque for £100,000 to the Lord Mayor of Sheffield for Warship Week in October 1941.

Dr W.H. Hatfield with horses at Brincliffe House in 1942.

Mr Webster's retirement in October 1942.

Staff group in a pantomime in January 1944.

The opening of 'Salute the Soldier Week' in June 1944. Here the 'daughter of the regiment' is selling savings stamps at the Firth Brown works.

Another image showing 'Salute the Soldier Week', 1944, with the 'daughter of the regiment' pictured with the Firth Brown band.

A publicity visit by 'starlet' Christine Nordon in December 1947. This photograph was taken in the melting department. The melter on the left is Bill Plackett.

A presentation to the winning apprentice of the year, Mr Wood, in November 1949. Eric Mensforth is seen here presenting the trophy. Charles Sykes sits in the background. The table is laden with books which were always given as prizes. A couple of the books here include *Domestic Hot Water Supplies* and *Calculus Made Easy*.

A Master Cutler's visit to Firth Brown's in 1950. The Master Cutler at the time was G. Wilton Lee. Eric Mensforth is seen walking in the centre. Walking through a steelworks would be slightly more restricted today.

Another picture of the Master Cutler's visit in 1950.

The Atlas and Norfolk Sports Club football team in November 1951.

Atlas and Norfolk Sports Club bowls team with trophies in April 1951. The building in the background is the old club house on Shirecliffe Road. This was eventually pulled down and replaced with a new one. On sports days a fair would set up behind the club house.

The Firth Brown Operatic Society in elaborate costume in May 1953.

A large group of staff pictured at a presentation to Mr Hancock in September 1953, presumably on his retirement from the firm.

A Firth Brown exhibition stand at the Engineering and Marine Exhibition in September 1953. Large rings and polished rolls are on show, together with photographs taken by Firth Brown photographers.

A close up picture of products at the Engineering and Marine Exhibition in 1955. The figure in the centre is Firth Brown's 'Atlas' emblem.

A Firth Brown and Firth Derihon exhibition stand at the Farnborough Air Show in 1958. During the 1950s Firth Brown exhibited at this show every year. The trade show was well attended and was an exhibition of everything associated with the aeronautical industry. Firth Brown usually filmed the air show.

The Firth Brown stand at the Engineering Materials and Design Exhibition in 1961. The man in the centre is Mr Brian Battersby, Director of Firth Derihon, Darley Dale.

The Firth Brown Tools Ltd '25 Club' at a dinner in November 1968.

Mr Jessel addressing a managers' dinner in 1973 in the staff dining room. Wilf Aram is on the right with Mr Evans(?) on the left. Bill Lapper has his back to the photographer.